Contents

Introduction

Before the 20th century, wall paintings were a common form of decoration and they can survive hidden beneath later covering layers or materials. This guidance offers practical advice on what to do if wall paintings are discovered, along with information on who to contact for assistance.

What is a wall painting?

Wall paintings may be defined as any painted design or composition applied directly to the surfaces of a building. Ranging from simple decorative patterns or imitations of other materials (such as stone or wood) to more complex figurative or narrative schemes, wall paintings are part of the building fabric.

Wall paintings are sometimes referred to as 'murals' or 'frescoes' and these terms have specific meanings which refer to their painting technique. For this reason, in this document the generic term 'wall painting' is used throughout.

1 The highly important paintings at the Byward Tower, Tower of London, show how expensive pigments (here, gold leaf and copper resinate) were used to decorate the finest interiors.

While some wall paintings can be simple in both design and technique, many are made up of a combination of materials applied as a succession of layers. These layers include, in most cases:

- **support** – the structural component of the building onto which the wall painting has been applied; it can be a single construction material, such as stone, or a composite structure, such as wattle-and-daub.

- **substrate** – a distinct intermediate layer that is often applied to the support, such as plaster or wooden panelling, to provide a finished surface for the painting.

- **paint layer(s)** – comprising pigments, both natural and manufactured, mixed with binding media, which can be water-based, oil-based or of glue made from organic materials (plant or animal). The paint can be applied in a single layer, or a succession of layers, and can include additional materials, such as metal leaf or low-relief attachments.

Paintings in ecclesiastical buildings

Most medieval church interiors in England were originally painted with extensive decorative and narrative schemes. Imagery within the church provided spiritual focus, and was used to express visual messages for those unable to read the Bible.

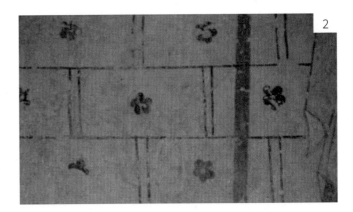

2 'Masonry pattern' – the decoration of plain plastered walls with lines in red (or sometimes simply incised) to imitate rows of ashlar masonry – can be found in medieval buildings throughout England from the 12th century. Often embellished with rosettes or other motifs, it was usually part of an overall scheme of decoration that covered all interior surfaces, and, in churches, would have featured narrative scenes as well.

3 Foliate scrollwork in red (pigment mostly lost), on a white background, typical of the 14th century. This type of modest decoration was used in churches and domestic settings, and often extended over stone, plaster and timber alike.

4 In the 19th century, the Victorians revived this interest in overall church decoration, using painting together with glass and other materials to fully decorate the interiors of their churches.

Paintings in secular buildings

While the existence of wall paintings in civic and other public buildings is reasonably well documented, there is an equally established tradition for the use of painted decoration within domestic buildings. Early medieval examples are extremely rare, and tend to be found within higher-status buildings that are already recognised through statutory protection. Most surviving wall paintings in modest vernacular buildings tend to date from the late 15th century onwards. Despite the increasingly widespread introduction of wallpapers in the 18th century (itself a significant form of historic decoration), the use of directly applied painted decoration has continued right up to the present day.

Both ecclesiastical and domestic paintings were subject to regular renovation and redecoration, often resulting in a complex layering of paint or polychromy.

5,6 In secular settings, wall paintings were often used to imitate more expensive architectural features, such as wooden panelling, marbled stone, or textile hangings. These examples show panelling (5) and wooden banisters (6).

Figures 7-9 : Understanding the date and significance of a wall painting
Identifying the date and subject matter of wall paintings can contribute to our understanding of a building's history and significance. A stylistic evaluation will look at painting technique, subject matter, costume, architectural elements, and distinctive details such as decorative motifs.

7 Wall paintings in the Agricola Tower, Chester Castle (*c.*1220). Although early documents had recorded the existence of wall paintings here, they were largely forgotten about – partly because they were obscured by a calcite 'veil'– and only rediscovered in the early 1990s during survey work. Their small-scale, fine technique and interesting subject matter (this scene shows the Visitation) is reminiscent of contemporary stained glass and manuscript illumination. Their rediscovery spurred an in-depth investigation into all of the wall surfaces within the building, and its possible connections with royal patronage.

8 These paintings at a house in Kent are typical of 16th-century 'grotesque' work, monochrome designs based on engravings that were known and widely disseminated throughout northern Europe. The use of engravings and 'pattern-books' was a popular way for owners to choose decoration and artists to gain inspiration.

9 These paintings at a house in Shropshire contain portraits of the owners. Their costume helped to pinpoint a date of around 1580, but the symbols in the painting were unusual – musical instruments, animals and flowers – and art-historical analysis indicated an allegorical painting of the Five Senses.

1 Concealed Wall Paintings

1.1 Why were wall paintings covered?

Wall paintings form the visible surface 'finish' to a building, and are therefore directly exposed to the effects of occupation and use. Over the course of many years, there may have been structural alterations to the building or redecoration due to shifts in fashion, religion and taste that resulted in the concealment or partial destruction of the wall paintings. Also, historic painted decoration will have suffered from general wear, as well as damage through environmental and event-driven decay. This may have prompted covering and successive redecoration (in similar or different styles), and the frequency of these changes can be extremely variable. The interior surface of a building can be made up of a complex sequence of layers and materials that provide an important and invaluable record, increasing our understanding of the building and its history.

In all cases, the circumstances surrounding the covering of wall paintings will have had a direct impact on their condition.

10

10 Wall paintings are often refurbished or completely covered over according to taste. At the Archer Pavilion, Wrest Park, close examination of the paintings in raking light reveals the faint raised pattern of brushstrokes relating to an earlier, more ornate, phase of decoration.

Ecclesiastical buildings

In the mid-16th century, most ecclesiastical wall paintings were obliterated as a result of the Protestant Reformation, a process that was repeated during the Civil War. Many paintings were physically destroyed, but it was also common to cover the earlier decoration with layers of limewash (or a new application of plaster), onto which acceptable – or less 'idolatrous' – decoration was applied. Though often much simpler in design, these post-Reformation paintings (usually texts) are of equal importance.

During the 18th and 19th centuries, extensive campaigns of church restoration brought a fashion for the stripping out of wall plasters. Conversely, the majority of newly constructed churches during this period saw a revival in elaborate painted decoration, using large firms of specialist decorators, who provided designs applied using either stencils or ready-made canvas paintings. Changing tastes in the 20th century saw these yet again covered over with simpler decoration.

There is also a long-standing tradition for the adaptation of ecclesiastical buildings for domestic use. In these instances, wall paintings are particularly vulnerable, since they are hidden and no longer linked to the way the building is currently being used.

Secular buildings

Domestic buildings can be highly deceptive: the true age of a building may be disguised because of building alterations over the years, such as extensions and 'updated' facades. This leaves original features hidden, and susceptible to unintentional damage.

11, 12 The façade of a building can be deceptive. This house appears to be Georgian, but its internal walls have medieval origins. Historical remodelling – including the insertion of a fireplace – cut directly through the wall paintings.

1.2 How were wall paintings covered?

Within the context of this guidance, 'covering materials' refer to any material – plaster, paint, limewash, or wood panelling, to name just a few – that hides the wall paintings from view. Technically, the covering system can be either direct or indirect.

Direct covering
Direct covering denotes any materials applied directly onto the painted surface. This can be additional paint or limewash layers (that may even include further painted decoration); later wallpapers (historic and modern); and layers of plaster or render.

Wall paintings covered by direct methods were often damaged by surface preparation (such as sanding or keying of the surface), causing permanent damage to the original decoration.

Indirect covering
Indirect covering denotes any system of covering that is not directly in contact with the painted surface. Examples of indirect covering include: forms of false lining (for example stud and plaster walling and suspended ceilings); blocking of decorated openings; wooden panelling; and fixed furniture.

There may be fixings driven directly through the wall (such as nails), resulting in localised damage that might weaken the substrate, making it even more vulnerable to deterioration.

13 'Keying', when plaster is hacked to improve the adherence of a new plaster layer, causes irreparable damage to wall paintings. When paintings are directly covered they are often damaged in this way.

14 Indirect covering can mean the insertion of nails into the walls to fix boarding.

2 Anticipating Wall Painting Discoveries

New discoveries of painted decoration within historic properties occur frequently across the country. Often, the discovery is purely accidental: during building works, or after specific events such as fire or flooding.

Lack of awareness of the potential for surviving historic decoration is largely to blame for inadvertent damage and loss. Moreover, when discoveries occur during building works, there are often both financial and scheduling pressures placed on any decision-making, and this can impact on the long-term care of wall paintings. A few steps can help to avoid damage when paintings are discovered.

15

16

15 Wall paintings were discovered after a fire in 2015 at this building in Suffolk. The building was virtually destroyed, revealing wall paintings on an internal gable wall (area outlined in red).

16 The paintings, mainly in black and white, could easily have been confused with soot, but close examination shows a band of text across the middle, with a figure on horseback above. The text included a date in the 17th century, consistent with the type of costume worn by the rider.

2.1 Where to expect wall paintings

It is safest to assume that all historic churches and most later medieval domestic buildings would have been decorated with wall paintings, and unless the wall structure or plaster has been removed, some painting is likely to survive. Therefore, anyone working in such buildings should expect wall paintings, extensive or fragmentary, to be present and act with the appropriate caution.

Understand the history of the building

Whether it is necessary for statutory consent, or as part of a general risk assessment for potential building works, the first step in assessing a historic property is always to find any existing information. This information might be in the form of written, graphic, and photographic records, as well as anecdotal evidence. Material relating to the property may be obtained through the local record office or public library. If the building is listed, the listing description (though these are often not exhaustive) can be useful. Other information from the local planning department may be available. It is also worth investigating the Historic England Archive, which holds a very large collection of photographs, drawings, reports and publications covering the whole country.

Place and street names, and even county boundaries, may have changed, so you may need to try a number of options for the property. It is also useful to check if any other similar buildings in the neighbourhood have wall paintings. For more information on how to research the history of your house see the Historic England website.

What consents do I need?

Ecclesiastical buildings

Buildings belonging to the Church of England, the Roman Catholic Church in England, the Methodist Church, the United Reformed Church, and the Baptist Union of Great Britain (when acting in the capacity of trustees) are managed under the Ecclesiastical Exemption (Listed Buildings and Conservation Areas) (England) Order 2010 but all other places of worship are treated under the Listed Building Consent regime, alongside secular buildings. See the Historic England website for information about the ecclesiastical exemption.

Secular buildings

This term covers all domestic, civic, and public buildings. It also includes those buildings used by all other religious denominations and faith groups that fall outside the Ecclesiastical Exemption Order. In many cases, buildings may have changed use, such as churches and chapels being converted for domestic occupation, and these are particularly vulnerable to internal damage through lack of awareness of their historic decoration. See the Historic England website for information on Listed Building Consent.

Be aware during building works

'Building works' may involve the alteration, repair or treatment of the building, both internally and externally. This can range from redecoration and routine maintenance to the renewal of building fabric or the insertion of building services (such as plumbing and electrics).

Where buildings are protected through statutory designation, such as listed buildings and scheduled monuments, works that can affect their special interest will be subject to statutory consent.

Undertaking a risk assessment before work starts can help anticipate areas of concern, greatly reducing the chances of accidental damage and wasted time and resources.

Contractors should be made aware of the risk of wall paintings being discovered in a building and the actions necessary in the event that they are found. The possibility of finding wall paintings, and the potential impact on the project, should always be included in the project's Risk Register.

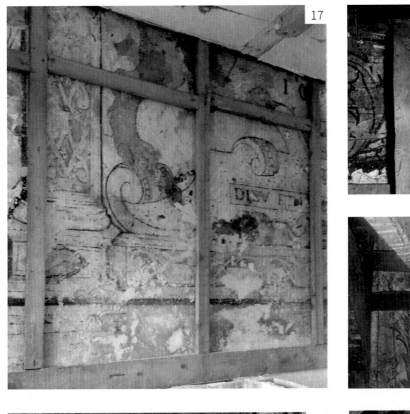

17–21 Paintings can be found during the insertion of services. They can be in fragmentary condition behind panelling, partition walls, and above later ceilings.

Look for telltale clues

A careful visual inspection can provide valuable clues to suggest the presence of covered wall paintings. These preliminary checks must be 'non-invasive', involving no physical interference with the wall surface, as this could put any underlying decoration at risk.

When looking at the internal surfaces, the presence of hidden decoration can be indicated by:

■ **Undulating surface texture and topography**
For plastered or rendered walls, an uneven or undulating surface may indicate the presence of older material behind it. Shining a strong light at an oblique angle across the surface of the wall ('raking light') may also reveal the texture of underlying brushstrokes (see Figure 10).

■ **Physical changes**
Looking carefully at both the exterior and interior of the building will help to identify any structural changes, such as extensions or the blocking of doorways and windows. Such changes are likely to have affected internal decoration, and they can be detected by visual clues such as disrupted cornicing or skirting boards. Small cupboards, new dividing walls or wooden panelling may conceal earlier painted surfaces.

Get specialist advice

The earlier a conservator is involved, the more likely it is that any 'at risk' decoration will survive. For advice on choosing and working with a conservator, see the Conservation Register on the Institute of Conservation's website. It is always worth checking with the local authority for potential financial assistance. A more accurate evaluation by a wall painting specialist may be necessary where:

■ the type or status of the building makes it likely that wall paintings survive

■ investigative research has found evidence that wall paintings are likely to survive

■ the building works are going to impact directly on the internal surfaces

■ it is a requirement, as part of the statutory conditions for consent

Consulting specialist archives can help establish the importance of newly discovered wall paintings. The National Survey of Medieval Wall Painting is one such archive, housed in the Conservation of Wall Painting Department at the Courtauld Institute of Art, London. It holds photographic and art-historical records of all known medieval wall paintings and pre-1800 domestic wall paintings in England, and new discoveries are regularly being made. To consult the survey, see their webpage.

3 Accidental Discovery

The condition of a newly uncovered painting can be fragile, as its constituent materials may respond to the sudden change in its environment. The removal of covering layers to reveal a wall painting not only means the irrevocable loss of later – possibly significant – layers, but also the exposure of the wall painting to further deterioration.

When paintings are found by accident, it is important to follow some simple guidelines.

3.1 Suspend building work

Ideally, the presence of historic decoration will have been established well in advance. This way, the building work can be organised to avoid potential damage.

When wall paintings are discovered during works, all activity in the affected area should be suspended temporarily until there is a detailed understanding of the nature and extent of surviving decoration. If a wall painting survives in one location, it is highly likely that it will extend to other surfaces within the room, or even other parts of the building. Extreme caution should therefore be taken. Even work that is not taking place in the immediate vicinity of the exposed wall painting may need to be reduced. Sensitive areas can be isolated, to lessen the risk of exposing or damaging further areas of painting.

Checklist
When historic painted decorations are discovered, it is important to:
■ suspend relevant building work, especially wet trades
■ stop uncovering the painting
■ record and collect any dislodged material
■ inform the relevant authorities
■ seek specialist advice

22

22 At the Anchor Inn, Sudbury (see Figures 15–16), the accidental discovery of wall paintings after a fire meant a halt to building works. Temporary protection was provided whilst specialist advice was sought. Full scaffolding with weather protection was installed at a later stage.

3.2 Stop uncovering the painting

Once historic decoration has been found, no further uncovering should take place until professional advice has been sought. Although it is very tempting to continue removing covering layers to reveal the scheme, such an intervention can be damaging, and can compromise options for treatment as well as increase costs for necessary conservation.

In addition, the nature of the later covering layers should be established to assess their own significance in the decorative history of the building, as these may merit preservation in their own right.

3.3 Record and collect material

If the area has been damaged in the course of the building works, there may be detached fragments of building material, such as fallen plaster or broken timber, which could retain painted decoration. This material may, in any case, hold archaeological information relevant to the assessment and treatment of the painting, and it is possible that it can be reinstated. It is therefore important to record where the fragments have come from, and to store them carefully for examination by a conservator.

When dealing with dislodged material, it is important to bear in mind the potential presence of asbestos; see the Health & Safety Executive for information.

Historic England recommends the use of accredited conservators who have obtained professional recognition through the Professional Accreditation of Conservator-Restorers (PACR) system. Within the United Kingdom, this scheme is operated through the Institute of Conservation (Icon). You can find an accredited conservator on their Conservation Register.

3.4 Inform the relevant authorities

Any decisions regarding the treatment of newly discovered wall paintings will have a direct impact on the fabric of the building. It is necessary to notify the local planning authority or the appropriate ecclesiastical authority at the earliest opportunity. Most local authorities employ a conservation officer, who offers expert advice on matters relating to historic buildings and they are an extremely useful point of contact. They will be able to advise you on whether you will need consent for any works that affect the wall paintings.

Early contact with the relevant bodies will help to clarify the relative significance of the decoration, provide specific conservation expertise, identify possible sources of funding, and help to locate and commission suitable specialists. For more information, see Where to Get Advice at the end of this document.

3.5 Seek specialist advice

In the case of a newly discovered wall painting, the advice of a specialist wall painting conservator is essential: as part of their conservation report, they will be able to clarify the extent and condition of the wall painting, offer guidance on its relative significance, and provide recommendations for its conservation.

The Conservation Register is a national database maintained by the Institute of Conservation containing details of accredited independent practices that provide specialist conservation services and support. The Register is designed to help potential clients to make informed choices. It offers advice on choosing and working with a conservator, and is available as a free searchable database on its website.

When asking for quotes, you should ask to see recent examples of the conservator's work to ensure you are confident with their proposals for treatment.

Proposals for treatment should build upon the information and material already collected about the building and its history, with a thorough on-site assessment of the nature and extent of surviving decoration, and the evaluation of its condition (the 'condition survey').

The conservator will produce a written report of the findings, providing detailed recommendations for further action, including the need for any additional investigations, any emergency stabilisation, and the medium and longer-term conservation requirements. For guidelines on conservation reports see the Historic England webpage.

Condition surveys

As part of the conservation report , the conservator will carry out a condition survey. Taking into account the building fabric (including its condition, the internal environment and surrounding topography), this helps identify any factors that are contributing to its deterioration. The findings of the condition survey must be documented, and this is usually done photographically and graphically. Should any invasive investigations be required, those should be recorded too.

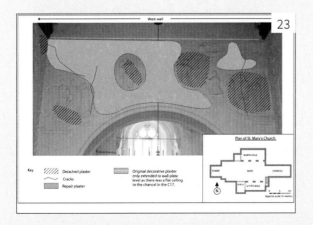

23 Condition surveys use graphic means to record the extent and condition of wall paintings.

What will a wall painting conservator do?

- Establish the nature and extent of the wall paintings

- Assess their current condition, and the causes of deterioration

- Identify published or unpublished records of the wall paintings where available

- Identify the need for any emergency remedial conservation, and any additional investigations necessary to clarify and assess deterioration factors

- Evaluate the conservation requirements of the site as a whole

- Propose conservation options, and check against agreed objectives as part of an integrated conservation programme

- Implement agreed conservation measures

- Agree future maintenance and management strategy

- Ensure all associated documentation is complete and copies lodged with all relevant parties, including the local Historic Environment Records (HERs)

3.6 Stabilise the wall paintings

In certain cases where the paintings are at immediate risk, emergency stabilisation may be required to safeguard them in the short term.

Any urgent remedial works that are necessary to secure the safety of the wall paintings would be conducted immediately, during the condition survey. This may be the case if the paintings are vulnerable, or when essential structural works need to continue in the building which put the paintings at risk. This can only be short-term, and must be built into any conservation treatment programme.

All emergency measures should be based on a clear method statement produced by the wall painting conservator. Emergency remedial works involve the direct treatment of painted surfaces (procedures such as inserting temporary plaster fills, emergency grouting or flake-fixing) and possibly the addition of temporary structural support. The work must be fully recorded, including all materials used, and be integrated within a plan for longer-term remedial treatment.

24 A conservator at work.
25 Emergency conservation measures. Small plaster fills covered with japanese tissue, used to stabilise cracks on this wall painting until treatment can continue.
26 Grouting (injecting a slurry, usually lime-based) into a wall painting to re-adhere the plaster to the substrate.

Specialist investigations

Sometimes a visual inspection (in diffuse or raking light) does not answer questions that a conservator may have. Specialist techniques can be a useful way to find out more about the painting and its condition.

However, with any form of specialist investigation it is vital that the questions – and the likelihood that a technique might answer them – are defined at the outset. There are myriad techniques available but they may not necessarily be useful or relevant.

The types of specialist techniques likely to be used in the conservation of wall paintings include those that aim to establish the extent of surviving paint, or the nature and stratigraphy of the paint layers. Investigation may also be required to identify the type of deterioration, or factors contributing to it, such as the environmental conditions.

Techniques should focus initially on non-invasive methods (infrared or ultraviolet light are examples of these) before using invasive methods that might involve the sampling of original material.

---

27 A faintly visible area of decoration on the stonework of this arch is obscured by a layer of paint.

28 The decoration can be seen clearly under infrared reflectography because pigments absorb wavelengths differently.

29 Thermal imaging was used in this building to understand the behaviour of the underlying materials and see patterns of moisture ingress.

30 The results show that the areas in blue are colder and associated with water penetration.

31 Taking 'spot' readings of envrionmental conditions with a hand-held meter can be useful to determine spatial variations and help plan more exact investigations.

32 Paint samples are used (this example is from the painting shown in Figure 1) to gain information on pigments (here showing the use of expensive verdigris and azurite) and to aid our understanding of the original painting techniques, informing future treatment.

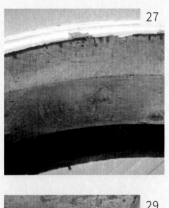

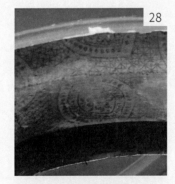

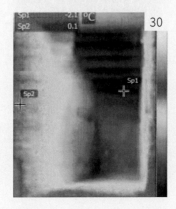

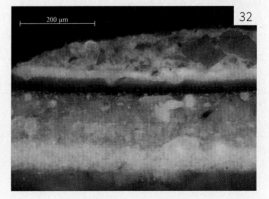

3.7 Protect the wall paintings

The presence and significance of the wall paintings should be formally brought to the attention of contractors on site and included in the induction of new contractors.

Where paintings are stable but building works need to continue elsewhere in the building, measures should be taken to minimise the risk to the paintings from any wet trades, dramatic variations in temperature and humidity levels, vibration, abrasion, and the deposition of airborne dust and debris. This may involve structural support to the wall or plaster, and a protective system. In rare cases, a temporary intervention layer is applied to the surface of the paintings.

If protective layers are left for too long, the facings are not only unsightly but they can become difficult to remove and may promote further deterioration. All treatment must be temporary and, more importantly, reversible.

For further information on the temporary protection of wall paintings during building works, see Historic England's webpage.

33

---

33 A temporary structure in the process of being erected to protect overmantel paintings from damage during building renovations.

3.8 Understand the conservation options

The wall painting conservator's report will form the basis for determining an agreed strategy for the conservation of any revealed wall paintings. This must be fully integrated within an overall conservation programme for the building.

In most cases, the options for the conservation of wall paintings can be divided into three main approaches: to conserve what has been found; to uncover; or to record and re-cover. A combination of these approaches, to suit the specific circumstances of the site, may sometimes be considered.

Conserve what has been found

The decision to conserve 'as found' is normally chosen where the future of the site has yet to be resolved. The conservator's role is to ensure that all areas where painted decoration survives are identified, and that all exposed areas of wall painting are stabilised where required. A clear description of the conservation work undertaken should be included in the final conservation report.

Direct physical markers to identify the survival of decoration will minimise the risk of future inadvertent damage. This approach may not offer the most aesthetically pleasing result, but allows for time to establish what needs to be done and obtain resources. The building must be properly repaired and maintained to ensure the long-term preservation and protection of all exposed areas of decoration.

Uncover

The decision to uncover wall paintings raises additional conservation issues. Partial or full uncovering of wall paintings may place the underlying material at risk, and will clearly sacrifice overlying layers, which are a part of the building's decorative history and may themselves be of some significance. Factors which support further uncovering include:

■ when the covering materials are actively contributing to the deterioration of the wall paintings

■ when concealment causes the risk of inadvertent damage to the paintings

■ when the remaining covering materials can be safely and effectively removed

■ as an interim measure to enable the conservation of the scheme prior to potential re-covering

■ when the paintings present a special aesthetic or historic value

In reaching a decision you need to consider:

■ To what extent do the wall paintings actually survive? Extremely fragmentary remains may not allow for an understanding of the decorative scheme.

■ How well have they been preserved? The paintings may have been scraped down or hacked before being covered over.

■ Are the current circumstances within the building appropriate for their exposure? Additional protective measures may be needed.

Costs for the uncovering and subsequent conservation have to be considered too. Uncovering can be a time-consuming and expensive undertaking and needs to be balanced against the resources available for the whole project.

34 Uncovering must only be carried out by an accredited wall painting conservator. This is an invasive process and can cause permanent damage to the paint layer.

Record and re-cover

In cases where further uncovering is deemed inappropriate, re-covering of the decoration may be the most effective means of protecting it against further damage or deterioration. Re-covering must only be undertaken by a wall painting conservator following detailed recording of the areas, and the methods used should aim to permit safe and effective removal in the future.

Where all areas of exposed decoration are to be concealed, it is essential that their presence is made clear in the documentation relating to the site, and this information must be readily available to those responsible for the property. It is important to retain easy access for future condition checks.

35

36

35,36 Two different ways that owners have decided to re-cover wall paintings in their homes, with a curtain (35) and wooden panelling (36).

4 Long-term Care

4.1 Effective building maintenance

Effective maintenance of the building is one of the most important factors in the preservation of internal decorative surfaces; regular checks of roofs, windows, rainwater goods and building services are essential. Combining a routine inspection of the building with visual monitoring of the wall paintings can help ensure that the wall paintings are maintained in the best possible condition.

37

---

37 In this case, wall paintings were discovered during renovation to convert the building into offices. This is not an ideal solution for vulnerable painted surfaces; careful use of the rooms and regular inspections are necessary to ensure their survival.

4.2 Monitor the condition of the paintings

Whether they are covered or exposed, wall paintings remain sensitive to their environment. In most cases, the owner-occupier or those in charge of the site are the people best placed to routinely review the condition of the wall paintings, and to monitor for any visible signs of change, especially if modifications have been carried out in the building (such as changes to the heating, or the use of the space). A good set of record photographs, along with location plans clearly identifying areas of surviving decoration, can be the most effective means of checking condition. Using this information as a guide, some of the signs to look out for include:

- new paint loss – fallen material at the base of the wall

- visual changes – such as darkening, surface bloom (white patches), or alterations of colour

- physical changes in the surface – such as bulging, cracking and flaking

- accumulation of excessive surface dust and dirt (including cobwebs)

Should any of these signs become evident, a wall painting conservator should be consulted.

5 Where to Get Advice

5.1 Historic England website

The Historic England website provides a wide range of advice for owners of historic buildings including how to get professional help, as well as links to various amenity societies who can offer advice on buildings of specific periods:
HistoricEngland.org.uk/advice/your-home

To obtain information and advice on places of worship, see:
HistoricEngland.org.uk/advice/caring-for-heritage/places-of-worship

Other technical information about wall paintings can also be found on our webpage:
HistoricEngland.org.uk/wallpaintings

5.2 Historic England publications

Practical Building Conservation series
This series of fully illustrated books published by Routledge provides detailed guidance on understanding deterioration, assessment and care and repair of historic buildings. Two of the volumes, *Mortars, Renders & Plasters* (2012) and *Earth, Brick & Terracotta* (2015) include specific information on wall paintings.

More information can be found at:
www.historicengland.org.uk/pbc

5.3 Sources of advice

For information on the conservation of wall paintings found in ecclesiastical buildings, see:
ChurchCare
Cathedral and Church Buildings Division
Church House
27 Great Smith Street
London SW1P 3AZ
www.churchcare.co.uk/churches/art-artefacts-conservation/caring-for-conservation-of-artworks-historic-furnishings/wall-paintings

For the National Survey of Medieval Wall Painting archive, contact:
Courtauld Institute of Art
National Survey of Medieval Wall Painting
Conservation of Wall Painting Department
Somerset House
Strand
London WC2R ORN
courtauld.ac.uk/research/sections/wall-painting-conservation/national-survey-of-medieval-wall-painting

To locate accredited conservators on the Conservation Register, see:
Icon
The Institute of Conservation
Unit 3.G.2, The Leathermarket
Weston Street
London SE1 3ER
www.icon.org.uk and
www.conservationregister.com

5.4 Contact Historic England

East Midlands
2nd Floor, Windsor House
Cliftonville
Northampton NN1 5BE
Tel: 01604 735460
Email: eastmidlands@HistoricEngland.org.uk

East of England
Brooklands
24 Brooklands Avenue
Cambridge CB2 8BU
Tel: 01223 582749
Email: eastofengland@HistoricEngland.org.uk

Fort Cumberland
Fort Cumberland Road
Eastney
Portsmouth PO4 9LD
Tel: 023 9285 6704
Email: fort.cumberland@HistoricEngland.org.uk

London
Fourth Floor
Cannon Bridge House
25 Dowgate Hill
London EC4R 2YA
Tel: 020 7973 3700
Email: london@HistoricEngland.org.uk

North East
Bessie Surtees House
41-44 Sandhill
Newcastle Upon Tyne NE1 3JF
Tel: 0191 269 1255
Email: northeast@HistoricEngland.org.uk

North West
3rd Floor, Canada House
3 Chepstow Street
Manchester M1 5FW
Tel: 0161 242 1416
Email: northwest@HistoricEngland.org.uk

South East
Eastgate Court
195-205 High Street
Guildford GU1 3EH
Tel: 01483 252020
Email: southeast@HistoricEngland.org.uk

South West
29 Queen Square
Bristol BS1 4ND
Tel: 0117 975 1308
Email: southwest@HistoricEngland.org.uk

Swindon
The Engine House
Fire Fly Avenue
Swindon SN2 2EH
Tel: 01793 445050
Email: swindon@HistoricEngland.org.uk

West Midlands
The Axis
10 Holliday Street
Birmingham B1 1TG
Tel: 0121 625 6870
Email: westmidlands@HistoricEngland.org.uk

Yorkshire
37 Tanner Row
York YO1 6WP
Tel: 01904 601948
Email: yorkshire@HistoricEngland.org.uk